Shaun the Sheep™

What a Mess!

Series Director: Richard (Golly) Goleszowski
Adapted by Monica Hughes

"Please put the rubbish in the bin, Bitzer," said the farmer.

Bitzer took the bag, but there was a rip in it.
The rubbish fell on to the grass.

There was a lot of rubbish!

Shaun put the rubbish in the bin.

The bin had wheels.
Shaun had a plan.

Shaun had lots of fun!

Crash!

The bin hit a tree.
The rubbish fell on to the grass.

Then Bitzer had a plan to suck up the rubbish.

Suck!

The rubbish went up, up, up.

Suck!
Suck!

Oops!

The rubbish went up ... but Shaun went up, too!

Bang!

"Is the rubbish in the bin yet?"
said the farmer.

No, it was not ...

but Shaun had a plan!